*Stroking
and gliding*

*Removing the
back brake*

A-stance

*Regaining
your balance*

Parallel turn

Heel stop

*Announcing
your intentions*

*Stepping
over a twig*

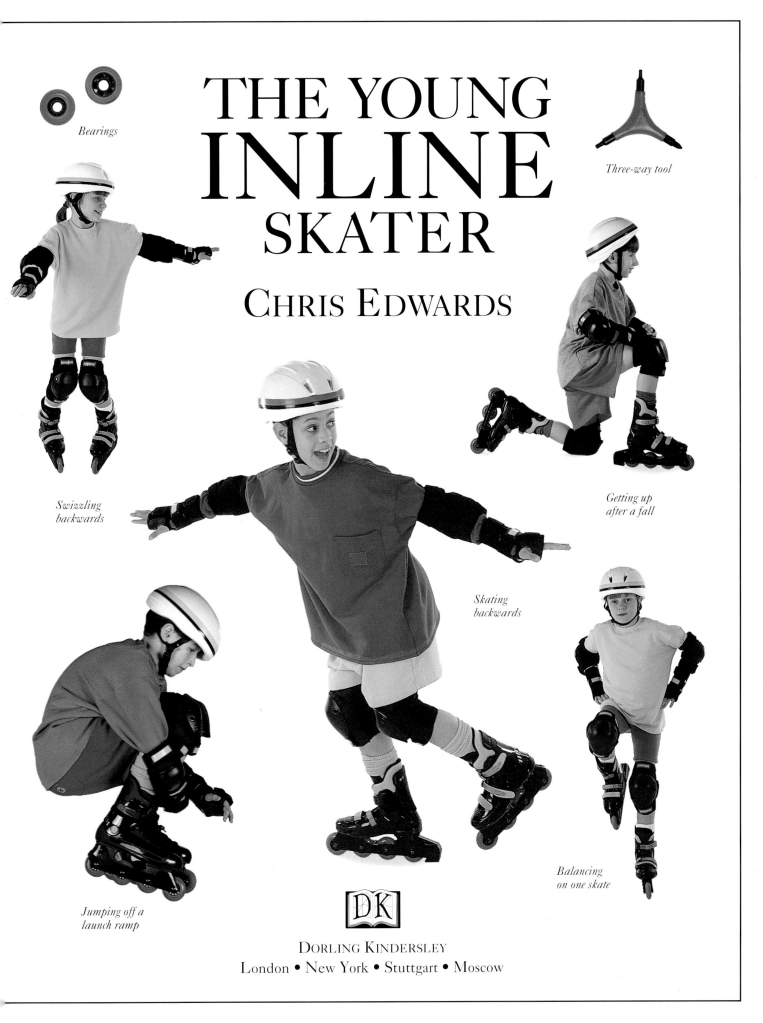

THE YOUNG
INLINE
SKATER

CHRIS EDWARDS

Bearings

Three-way tool

Swizzling backwards

Getting up after a fall

Skating backwards

Jumping off a launch ramp

Balancing on one skate

DK

DORLING KINDERSLEY
London • New York • Stuttgart • Moscow

A DORLING KINDERSLEY BOOK

Project Editor Fiona Robertson
Art Editors Cheryl Telfer & Rebecca Johns
Photography Ray Moller
Picture Research Helen Stallion
Production Charlotte Traill
Managing Editor Jane Yorke
Managing Art Editor Chris Scollen

The young inline skaters
James Hall, Simeon Hartwig, Barry Lee Normah, Peter Royal, and Kelly Wiles

Dorling Kindersley would like to thank Bauer for supplying
all the skates and protective gear used in this book.

First published in Great Britain in 1996
by Dorling Kindersley Limited
9 Henrietta Street, London WC2E 8PS

A CIP catalogue record for this book is available from the British Library.

ISBN 0-7513-5456-2

Colour reproduction by Colourscan, Singapore
Printed and bound in Italy by L.E.G.O.

Contents

To all young inline skaters

"THERE IS NOTHING more exhilarating than catching some big air over a half pipe ramp. Yet there is a lot more to inline skating than wild stunts. Inline skating is about physical fitness, good sportsmanship, discipline, and hard work. As with any sport, you have got to have the right equipment, the patience to learn the basic skills, and the time to practise as much as you can, so that you can be at your best in performance, competition, or in the park. It doesn't matter where you skate, it's how you skate. If you put in the effort, the rewards of this sport can be terrific. The videos, films, and Team Rollerblade® activities that I have been able to participate in have more than compensated for all the hours of hard work. I hope this book will inspire you and get you rolling! "

"I started skating when I was 13 years old. I knew right away inline skating was going to become a favourite pastime - even a career!"

"Some tricks, such as the Mute Grab that I'm doing here, are performed off a platform called a launch box."

"This trick is called a Japan Air. It takes a lot of momentum to propel yourself up this high. You need to build up terrific speed on the take-off to get this move off the ground."

"The Frontside Grind is another fun stunt, but remember you should never try any of these tricks without proper safety equipment and instruction. They might look effortless here, but they require lots of practice!"

"The Sad Plant Invert is one of my favourite tricks. It has it all – speed, height, power, and grace. Hang on to your helmets, because you're in for quite a ride with this freewheeling manoeuvre!"

History of inline skating

THE FIRST ROLLER, or "quad", skate was developed in the 1700s by a Belgian called Joseph Merlin. Merlin was a keen ice skater and wanted to develop a way of skating during the warm summer months. His idea of attaching wooden spools to his shoes seemed ingenious, but he could not turn or stop, so he fell many times! The first inline skate was developed in France in 1819, followed in 1823 by a five-wheeled invention by Englishman Robert John Tyers. However, turning and stopping were still a problem, and because the skates were made of iron, they were extremely unstable. The modern inline skate was developed in the 1980s by two American ice hockey players, Scott and Brennan Olson. Unlike the early models, today's skates are fast, smooth, and lightweight.

A fashionable hobby
Ice skating was used as a means of transport in Scandinavia as far back as 1100 BC, but it was not until the early 19th century that it became a popular and fashionable pastime.

A competitive edge
Roller-skating became much easier after the invention of wheel bearings in 1884. By 1947, it began to feature in competitions, such as this women's race in America.

A perfect fit?
Imagine how uncomfortable this skate from 1879 must have been. It is made from a high heeled shoe with wheels fitted underneath and a strap around the ankle.

Early roller-skating rink
The roller rink shown here was built at Crystal Palace, in London, in 1890. The floor was wooden and the rink was long and narrow, rather like skating rinks today. Skaters wore iron quad skates, with two wheels on either side of the skate boot.

The iron wheels had no bearings and were probably noisy and difficult to get rolling.

Early inline skate
Early inline skates had just two iron wheels and a leather strap to go around the ankle and lower leg. Because there was no heel brake, turning and stopping were very difficult!

The front stopper shown here has now been replaced by a back heel brake.

Modern inline skate
Scott and Brennan Olson, two devoted ice hockey players from Minneapolis, USA, developed the first modern inline skates, which they called "Rollerblades®". Their design was based on that of an ice hockey skate.

Starting out

INLINE SKATING IS one of the most exciting, fastest-growing sports today. It's also fun and easy to learn. The most important piece of equipment is your skates, which must fit properly and be comfortable. You should also ensure that you have the correct safety gear, to protect you from injury. Layers of loose, comfortable clothes that allow plenty of movement are ideal for skating in.

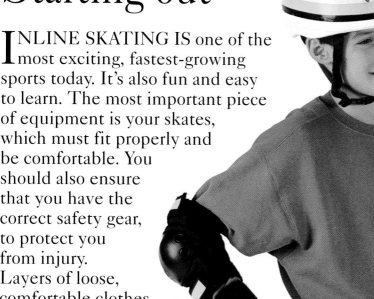

Most helmets have foam pads and adjustable straps to ensure a good fit.

A long-sleeved top will protect your skin if you fall.

Helmet
The helmet is the most important part of your safety gear. It must comply with safety standards, and fit your head securely and comfortably.

Elbow pads
Elbow pads offer valuable protection for your sensitive elbow joints. Like knee pads, they should be worn with the holes pointing downwards.

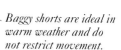

The plastic bump on the wrist guard should be under your palm.

Wrist guards
Hands and wrists are the areas most likely to get injured in a fall. Wrist guards have sturdy plastic pieces on the underside to protect against this.

A money-belt is useful for carrying small items such as keys or change.

Before you buy them, make sure that your skates fit properly and are supportive, particularly around the ankle.

Baggy shorts are ideal in warm weather and do not restrict movement.

A tight fit
Both elbow and knee pads have an elastic sleeve which fits over your arm or leg, and is secured with Velcro ®. Don't fasten them too tightly, or this could restrict your movements when skating.

Knee pads
Try to wear knee pads that have a fabric cushion covered by a hard plastic cup. The cushion absorbs the impact of a fall, and the plastic protects your skin and clothes.

A frame at the bottom of the skate holds the wheels in place. Most frames are about 30 cm (12 in) long.

Night gear

When skating at night, you must ensure that you can be clearly seen by motorists, cyclists, and pedestrians. It is often colder at night, so you should also dress warmly.

Wear a scarf or a top with a polo neck to keep your neck warm.

A warm, light-coloured jacket is ideal for skating at night.

A reflective strap or waistcoat is very important when skating at night because it allows people in front of you and behind you to see you.

If you are wearing gloves, put them on under your wrist guards.

Tracksuit bottoms are ideal for chilly evenings.

Be careful not to tighten the ankle strap too much, or you will not be able to skate correctly.

Tighten the middle strap the most so that your foot feels secure.

Heel brake

Inline skates

Most inline skates have a hard outer shell and a soft inner liner for support and comfort. The skates can be tightened with laces or buckles, or both. The right skate usually has a heel brake.

Leave the toe strap loose to avoid getting cramp.

Different types of wheel

Wheels

Your wheels have the greatest effect on your performance. Wheel sizes are measured in millimetres. The bigger the wheel, the faster it will go. Wheels also come in varying degrees of hardness, called durometer, ranging from 74A to 93A. The lower the durometer, the softer the wheel.

Reflective strips can be attached to your wrist pads.

Be seen

A good cycle shop should stock all the lights and reflective strips that you need.

Knee pads often have reflective strips sewn on to the Velcro® straps.

Skate light

Helmet light

It is extremely important to be visible from behind when you skate at night. Attach a light to an elastic strap around your helmet.

Skate light

Use a reflective Velcro® strap to attach a light to your skate. This will help to prevent it bouncing off when you hit a bump.

Skate smart

THE INTERNATIONAL INLINE Skating Association (IISA) is the governing body of inline skating. It has developed a public safety awareness campaign called Skate Smart. The aim of the campaign is to develop a set of rules for skaters that will allow them to enjoy the sport safely and without injury to themselves or others. Understanding and practising Skate Smart not only sets a good example, it encourages others to try this growing sport by promoting inline skating as a fun, safe activity.

Rules of the road
1. Always wear protective gear – helmet, knee and elbow pads, and wrist guards.
2. Learn the basic skills in a safe, flat area.
3. Keep your skates in good condition.
4. Stay alert and be courteous at all times.
5. Control your speed and be aware of changing conditions and hazards.
6. Obey all traffic regulations.
7. Do not skate in areas with heavy traffic.

Basic inline equipment
It is a good idea to put together a skate repair kit which you can carry in your skate bag. Make sure you buy the correct tools for your skates. Some general tools are shown below. Check with your local skate shop for more specialized tools.

Tool bag

Three-way tool *Bearings* *Container for spare bearings*

A selection of different Allen keys

Carrying your gear
In addition to your tools, you may want to carry other items, such as some money and a drink. You could use a personal stereo bag for this purpose, and a skate bag for your skates.

Tool bag to fit around boot *Skate bag*

Indicate your intentions clearly so that other skate are not taken by surprise.

Announce your intentions
Always overtake pedestrians, cyclists, and other skaters on the right. Announce your intentions by saying, for example, "Passing on your right". Overtake only when it is safe and you have enough room to do so.

Always stop and allow pedestrians to pass.

Pedestrian awareness
Always give way to pedestrians. It is polite and shows that you are safety conscious. Be a goodwill ambassador for inline skating.

Skate care

Skates actually require very little maintenance and any repairs that you do need to carry out tend to be fairly inexpensive. Keep your skates clean by wiping them occasionally with a soft, damp cloth. The most important part to check is the wheels. Look at them once a week for wear on the inside edges. Spin each wheel to make sure it is moving freely and listen for any grinding or gritty sounds that suggest the bearings are dirty.

Hold your skates at eye level to check them.

Changing wheels

1 Whether you are rotating an existing set of wheels, or replacing them with a completely new set, it is useful to know how to change your wheels. Hold the skate firmly between your legs and use the appropriate Allen key to unscrew the wheel bolt.

Insert the Allen key into the bolt to unscrew it.

2 Work on one wheel at a time. When you have unscrewed the bolt, remove it and lift out the wheel. To replace the wheel, insert it back into the frame and tighten each bolt as far as you can. When all the wheels are back in place, adjust each bolt slightly so that each wheel spins for the same length of time.

Lift the whole wheel out.

Wheel rotation

Rotating your wheels means changing their position on the skate frame and turning the wheels over so that their edges wear evenly. Inside wheel edges wear out more quickly than those on the outside edges, so rotating them makes them last longer.

The arrows show the positions to which the wheels move after they have been rotated.

④ ③ ② ①

Wheel rotation chart

Number the wheel positions from front to back, so that the toe wheel is number one, as shown above. Following the chart shown right, move wheel number one to position number three on the other skate; wheel number two becomes number four, and so on until all the wheels have been rotated.

Old position on skate	New position on other skate
1 →	3
2 →	4
3 →	1
4 →	2

Cleaning and replacing bearings

Each skate wheel has two sets of tiny round metal bearings. These enable the wheel to spin smoothly. The condition of your bearings has a tremendous effect on the speed at which you skate. Dirt in your bearings not only slows you down, it will also destroy the bearings eventually. Most bearings are sealed inside a casing which is designed to repel dirt, but if you do skate through dust, sand, or water, it's best to clean them straight away.

1 The outer bearings casing tends to attract a lot of dust. You should wipe it down regularly with a dry cloth or a clean paper towel. A toothbrush is also useful for cleaning inside the grooves.

2 To clean or change all the bearings, use a three-way tool (see page 12) to pop the bearings out on both sides. Clean the bearings with a dry cloth, but don't oil them. When you replace them, be careful not to tighten the bolt too much.

Removing the back brake

Back brakes can be either square or round. When your brake has worn below the halfway mark, you should either replace it (if it is the square brake), or turn it around to expose more rubber (if it is the round brake).

Remove the back brake in the same way as the wheels. Make sure you use the correct Allen key.

Hold the skate firmly between your legs.

Warming up

INLINE SKATING IS a very physical activity which uses lots of muscles in your body. Before you put your skates on, it is therefore important to spend time stretching and warming up. This will help to stop you injuring yourself and will also make you feel more relaxed and confident when you skate. The stretches shown here will loosen the major muscles used while skating.

Hamstring stretch

To stretch the large hamstring muscle at the back of your thigh, lie on your back with one knee bent. Raise the other leg in the air. Hold the leg behind your knee and gently pull it back.

Try to keep this leg slightly bent to ensure you stretch the muscle.

Make sure you keep this foot on the floor.

Keep your back straight.

Hamstring and calf stretch

Placing your hands on your left thigh for support, bend your left leg and extend your right leg out in front of you. Push your hips backwards until you feel a stretch in the hamstring at the back of your right thigh. If you lift your toe, you will also feel a stretch in your calf, or lower leg, muscle.

Lift up your toe to increase the stretch.

This leg should be bent for support.

Side bends

With your feet apart and your knees bent, reach one arm into the air and stretch over to the other side. Remember to stretch up from your waist. Keep your hips steady and facing forwards. Hold the stretch for 20 seconds and then repeat on the other side.

Try not to lean forwards as you stretch up.

Double-sided
All of these stretches should be repeated on your other side, too.

Place this hand on your hip.

Bend your knees slightly.

Arm circling

Your arms should be close to your ears.

Don't forget to swing your arms forwards, too.

Try to breathe normally throughout this exercise.

1 Stand up straight with your knees slightly bent. Raise your arms straight out in front of you.

2 Keep your arms straight and bring them above your head as you start to circle them backwards.

3 Finish the circle by bringing your arms backwards and down to the sides. Repeat 10 times.

Time scale
Hold each stretch for about 15-20 seconds.

Gluteal stretch
Lie on your back and cross your right foot over your left knee. Raise your left leg and hold the back of your left thigh. Feel a stretch in your right hip.

Place this foot over your left knee.

Lift this foot off the ground.

Hip flexor
Bend your right knee and extend your left leg behind you. Lean forwards by bending your front knee more and feel a stretch in the front of your left hip.

Place your hands on your thigh for balance.

Quadriceps stretch
The quadriceps, or thigh muscle, is one of the main muscles used in inline skating. To stretch it, stand on one foot with your supporting knee bent. Pull back the other foot towards your bottom. Keep your knees together and push your hips forwards.

Keep your knees together.

Extend this leg back.

Inner thigh stretch
Sit on the ground and extend both legs to the side. Keep your shoulders relaxed and your head up. Lean forwards from your waist, keeping your hands on the ground.

Lean forwards slightly more when you feel the tension in your muscles begin to ease.

If you are not very flexible at first, stretch your inner thigh by pulling the soles of your feet together like this.

Hold on to your feet.

Smooth stretching
When stretching, it is important never to bounce or jerk the muscle. Try to breathe normally.

This stretches your outer thigh muscle.

Outer thigh stretch
Sit on the ground with your left leg straight out in front of you and cross your right foot over it. Press your left elbow against your right thigh and feel the stretch in the muscle.

Upper back stretch
Link your fingers and push both arms out in front of you. Feel a stretch in between your shoulder blades.

Push your arms forwards.

Easy does it
Only stretch until you feel tension in the muscles, not pain.

Bend your knees.

Don't lock your elbows.

Chest stretch
The opposite of the stretch above is the chest stretch. Simply take both arms behind you and clasp your hands. As you pull your arms upwards, you will feel a stretch at the front of your shoulders and across your chest.

Ready to roll

NOW THAT YOU HAVE your skates and protective gear on, it's time to get started. The first thing you need to learn is how to stand correctly. This will help you to keep your balance, which in turn will improve your confidence. Practise at first on a patch of grass so that your skates do not roll out of control. Try to stay relaxed and always remember to keep your head up and your eyes focused on the route ahead – not on your skates!

Edges

Look straight down your wheels. You will see that the middle of the wheel is flat and the sides are sloping. These are your wheel edges.

Push your ankles outwards.

Your feet should be shoulder-width apart.

Centre edges
The flat part of the wheel is the centre edge. Shuffle your skates back and forth, and you will be on your centre edges.

Outside edges
With your feet together, push your ankles outwards. You are on your outside edges. With experience, you will use your outside edges more.

The ready position

Every move in inline skating starts and finishes with the ready position. In this position, your upper body, legs, and arms should be balanced and centred over your skates. This helps you to control your skates, whatever your speed and conditions.

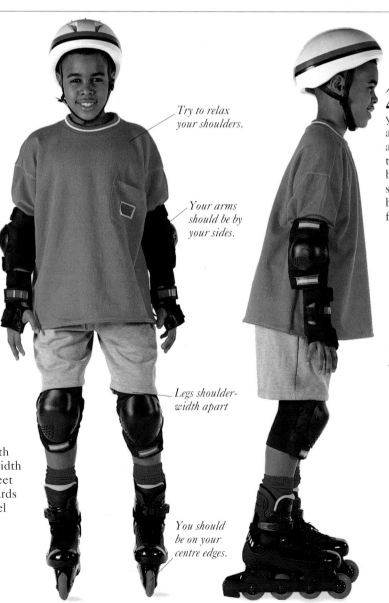

Try to relax your shoulders.

Your arms should be by your sides.

Legs shoulder-width apart

You should be on your centre edges.

1 Stand on a flat, smooth surface with your feet shoulder-width apart. Shuffle your feet backwards and forwards to get used to the feel of the wheels rolling beneath you.

2 Stand completely straight, with your head up, your arms by your sides, and your legs together. Without bending at the waist, slowly lean your body forwards from your ankles.

Bend slightly from your waist.

Bend your knees.

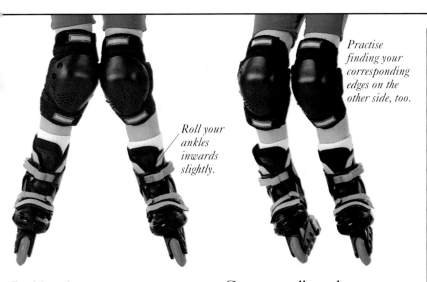

Practise finding your corresponding edges on the other side, too.

Roll your ankles inwards slightly.

Inside edges

When you stand with your feet wider than your shoulders, you are on your inside edges. Inside edges are used a lot in skating, especially when moving forwards.

Corresponding edges

With your feet about 15 cm (6 in) apart, push your left ankle inwards and your right ankle outwards. These are your corresponding edges, which you use when you turn.

Stances

When you are confident in the ready position, try these different feet positions, or stances. Remember to keep your knees bent, your head up, and your arms out in front of you.

V-stance

When you take your first skating step, you will start from the V-stance. Stand with your feet together and your toes turned outwards. Roll your wheels onto their inside edges.

Inside edges

A-stance

When you first learn to turn, you will use the A-stance, in which your feet are wider than your shoulders, to help you feel more stable. You should be on your inside edges.

Inside edges

3 Now bend your knees and repeat the movement until you can feel your shins pressing against the tongues of your skates. If you look down, you should only be able to see the tops of your knee pads. Try to bend slightly from your waist, too.

Nose to toes
In this position, try to keep your nose, knees, and toes in a straight line.

Keep looking ahead.

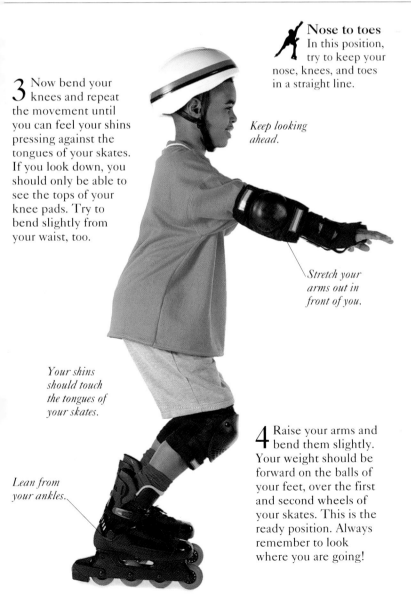

Stretch your arms out in front of you.

Your shins should touch the tongues of your skates.

Lean from your ankles.

4 Raise your arms and bend them slightly. Your weight should be forward on the balls of your feet, over the first and second wheels of your skates. This is the ready position. Always remember to look where you are going!

Scissor stance

You will use this stance to glide, stop, and turn. With your feet about 15 cm (6 in) apart, shuffle one skate in front of the other until the back wheel of the front skate is beside the front wheel of the back skate.

Front wheel   *Back wheel*

Stroke and glide

INLINE SKATING IS about movement, which you have to create. The best way to move forwards is with an action called stroking and gliding. One skate strokes outwards and slightly back, which pushes you forwards, while the other skate glides, or coasts, along the ground. Together, these two movements create a "stride". Remember to use small strokes when you first start out.

Stroke practice

Stand in the ready position (see page 17) with your feet in a V-stance. Imagine that your feet are the hands on a clock face – your right skate points to 1 o'clock and your left skate points to 11 o'clock.

Lean forwards slightly in the direction that you are moving.

Keep your knees bent.

Roll your ankle inwards.

Inside edge

1 From the V-stance, gently push your right skate out to the side and then return it to the V. Repeat this move with the left skate to get used to the feel of your wheels rolling beneath you.

Push with your back leg.

Advanced striding

When you become more experienced at stroking and gliding, you can adjust your body position to give you more control over your skates. For example, note the low body position and flat back adopted by the skater in this picture.

Skate style
Roll your right skate outwards. Your left skate should be on its inside edge as you prepare to push off.

Glide on your right foot.

Push off with the left foot.

2 Shift your weight to your right foot as you push off, or stroke, with your left skate. Let your right skate glide forwards along the ground and lift your left skate off the ground. This is your first stride!

Skate style
The stroke of the left skate propels you forwards. As it lifts off the ground, the right skate glides along the surface.

Finding your balance

Being able to balance on one foot is not only vital to stroking and gliding, it is also a necessary skill to master before you try any more advanced moves, such as crossover turns (see pages 26-27).

One-leg balance

Practise balancing on each foot by standing in the ready position and picking up one foot at a time. See how long you can stand on one leg.

Your arms should be outstretched.

Duck walk

This exercise will prepare you for your first striding steps. Your feet should be in a V-position, with your toes pointed outwards and your wheels on their inside edges. Pick up each foot and take small steps forwards.

Swizzles

Swizzling, or sculling, is another way of skating forwards. It can be done slowly or at speed. Learning to swizzle will enable you to swerve and turn, avoid obstacles, and generally be more in control of your skates.

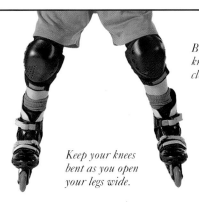

Keep your knees bent as you open your legs wide.

Bring your knee pads close together.

Constant contact
Your feet should not leave the ground at all during swizzling.

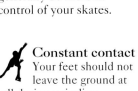

1 Stand with your heels together and your toes apart. Bend your knees and roll on to your inside edges.

2 Push your skates outwards by opening your legs wide. This will get you rolling forwards. Keep your weight on the balls of your feet.

3 Point your toes inwards and pull your feet together again until they are back in their starting position.

Keep your head up.

Always look where you are going.

You should always be able to see your arms. This way, your weight will stay forwards.

Glide in the ready position between strokes.

Centre edges

3 Bring your feet together and coast along on the centre edges of both skates while you recover your balance. You should be in the ready position, with your weight on the balls of your feet. This position is called parallel rolling.

Push your shin up against the tongue of your boot as you glide along on your left skate.

Speed skating
The more confident you become, the faster you will want to go. Using your arms will help you pick up speed. Swing them from side to side in time with your strides, as shown above.

Good posture
Remember to bend from your knees, lean from your waist, and keep your head up.

4 Try the stroke-and-glide action again, this time pushing off with your right foot and gliding along on your left skate. Continue balancing on one foot while you push off with the other, making sure you return to parallel rolling each time. When you feel confident, try linking the strokes together.

How to stop

BEFORE YOU LEARN to go much faster on your skates, it is vital that you are able to stop safely. Stopping is not difficult, but it may feel awkward at first and requires plenty of practice. There are many ways to decrease your speed and stop on inline skates, but the heel brake is the first and most efficient method you will use. Most inline skates come with a heel brake already fitted. It is usually on the right skate, but can be moved to the left if you are left-handed. The brake is square or round and is usually made of rubber.

Look ahead, not down at your skates.

Keep your arms out to maintain balance.

Lean forwards slightly at the waist to put more body weight and pressure on the brake.

Heel stop

The first type of braking system developed for inline skates was the heel stop and it is probably still the most effective. Make sure you practise on grass first before moving to a flat, rolling surface.

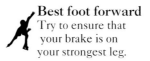

Best foot forward
Try to ensure that your brake is on your strongest leg.

1 Glide forwards in the ready position and scissor your feet so that your braking foot is in front. The brake should be beside the front wheel of your back skate.

2 Lift the toe of your braking skate until you can feel the brake on the ground. Don't stop suddenly – glide forwards and increase the pressure on the brake gradually.

3 When the braking skate is in position, bend your back knee as you glide along. This will make you feel as though you are sitting back and will give you more control of the brake.

Spin stop

Like the T-stop (see page 21), the spin stop is a way of stopping without using your heel brake.

1 This sequence shows a spin to the right. From a ready position, place your right skate behind and lift up your heel. Keep the front wheel gliding along the ground.

Make sure the front wheel of this skate remains on the ground.

Your arms should be in front of you.

Open your arms out to the side to help you balance.

2 Turn your right knee outwards by pivoting on your front wheel. This will force your legs open and your left foot will start to turn.

Your feet should be in a scissored stance (see page 17).

3 Set your right skate down on the ground. Keep your heels together and your knees bent. Now both skates will be travelling into the spin. Keep your arms to the side and your chest up to stop yourself falling forwards.

Keep gliding along on this foot.

Set this skate down with your heels together.

T-stop

1 The T-stop does not use the heel brake. Instead, as its name suggests, you stop by making your skates form the shape of a capital "T". Glide forwards in the ready position. Your skates should be in a scissor stance with the braking foot behind.

Braking foot   *Scissor stance*

2 Keep your body weight centred over the front leg (here, the left leg). Slowly turn the toe of your back skate outwards. You will feel the wheels on this skate start to drag along the ground on the inside edge.

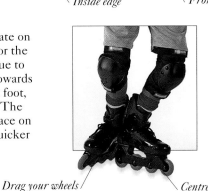

Inside edge   *Front leg*

3 Keep the front skate on either the centre or the outside edge. Continue to drag your back foot towards the heel of your front foot, to form a "T" shape. The more pressure you place on your back foot, the quicker you will stop.

Drag your wheels along the ground.   *Centre or outside edges*

Wear and tear
The main disadvantage of the T-stop is that you use your inside edges to stop. This makes your wheels wear out more quickly than usual.

Hold this arm out for balance.

Bring one arm across your chest to stop you spinning around.

Keep both knees bent.

4 It is very important to bend both knees as you stop. Try not to turn the back skate too far to the side, otherwise you will spin. To prevent this happening, bring the arm that is on the same side as your back leg across your body (here, the right arm). Hold the other arm out to the side to help you balance.

Slowly does it
Only use this stop when you are travelling slowly, or to stop yourself falling.

Don't forget to practise this stop to the left, too.

Keep your head and chest up to stop you falling forwards.

4 Your skates will automatically complete the spin, and you will stop. Although this technique may feel uncomfortable at first, with lots of practice, it will get easier.

Power slide

The power slide is one of the most impressive ways to stop. However, it is also dangerous so you must wear full protective gear.

1 Keep your body weight centred over the front leg (here, the left leg). Slowly lift your back skate and turn the toe outwards.

2 Replace your back foot on the floor in a sliding position. Make sure you angle this foot so that you slide on the inside edges of your wheels rather than your skate frame. Your upper body should be facing in the same direction as your front skate.

Falling safely

A T SOME POINT, every skater experiences the feeling of losing his or her balance or catching a wheel, and tumbling to the ground. Don't worry – falling is part of the fun of learning and the key to a safe landing is knowing how to fall and how to get up. The more relaxed you are, the less likely you are to injure yourself. Never try to fight a fall by grabbing at trees, fences, or even people. Instead, trust in your protective gear and try to stay calm.

Try to lean forwards when you feel yourself starting to fall.

Bend at the waist.

Don't lock your elbows.

Keep your knees bent.

1 Experienced skaters usually fall quickly because they are travelling so fast. However, as a beginner, you will be travelling much more slowly, and can therefore often feel yourself starting to fall. Always try to fall forwards if possible. Try to stay relaxed, and lower your centre of gravity by bending at the waist.

Geared up
It's very important that you wear your protective gear correctly. The elastic sleeve must go around the backs of your knees and elbows. It is then tightened with the Velcro® straps.

Getting up from a fall

Falling down on the ground is the easy part. However, learning how to get up properly will stop you sliding back down into your original position. This may be entertaining for people watching, but won't help you much!

Bring this leg over as you roll on to your side.

1 Begin by rolling on to your back and then your side. Start to push yourself up with your hands.

How to fall

If you have ever watched a game of ice hockey, you will have noticed that the players seldom hurt themselves when they fall. This is because they slide along the ice, which reduces the impact of the fall. The plastic on your protective gear acts in a similar way, allowing you to slide along the ground.

Try to fall on to your knees first.

2 As you hit the ground, try to direct the impact of the fall on to your protective gear by landing first on your knees, then your elbows, and lastly your wrists. Keep your fingers up to avoid grazing your knuckles.

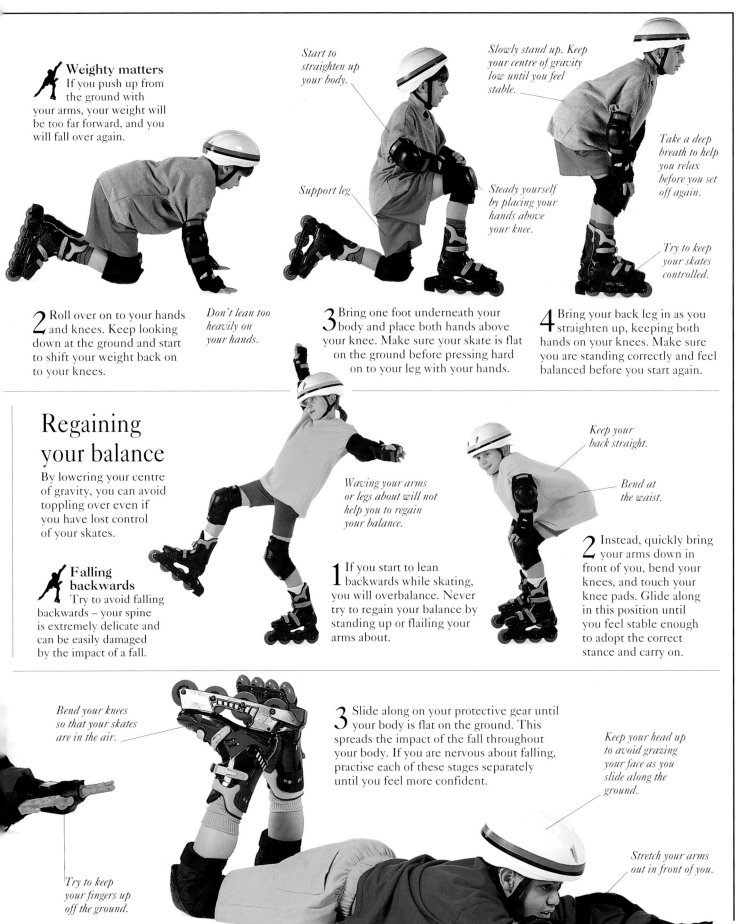

Weighty matters
If you push up from the ground with your arms, your weight will be too far forward, and you will fall over again.

Start to straighten up your body.

Slowly stand up. Keep your centre of gravity low until you feel stable.

Support leg

Steady yourself by placing your hands above your knee.

Take a deep breath to help you relax before you set off again.

Try to keep your skates controlled.

2 Roll over on to your hands and knees. Keep looking down at the ground and start to shift your weight back on to your knees.

Don't lean too heavily on your hands.

3 Bring one foot underneath your body and place both hands above your knee. Make sure your skate is flat on the ground before pressing hard on to your leg with your hands.

4 Bring your back leg in as you straighten up, keeping both hands on your knees. Make sure you are standing correctly and feel balanced before you start again.

Regaining your balance

By lowering your centre of gravity, you can avoid toppling over even if you have lost control of your skates.

Falling backwards
Try to avoid falling backwards – your spine is extremely delicate and can be easily damaged by the impact of a fall.

Waving your arms or legs about will not help you to regain your balance.

1 If you start to lean backwards while skating, you will overbalance. Never try to regain your balance by standing up or flailing your arms about.

Keep your back straight.

Bend at the waist.

2 Instead, quickly bring your arms down in front of you, bend your knees, and touch your knee pads. Glide along in this position until you feel stable enough to adopt the correct stance and carry on.

Bend your knees so that your skates are in the air.

3 Slide along on your protective gear until your body is flat on the ground. This spreads the impact of the fall throughout your body. If you are nervous about falling, practise each of these stages separately until you feel more confident.

Keep your head up to avoid grazing your face as you slide along the ground.

Try to keep your fingers up off the ground.

Stretch your arms out in front of you.

Turns

WHETHER YOU WANT TO change direction, negotiate a corner, steer around hazards or other skaters, or simply stop, knowing how to turn is an invaluable skill to learn. Turns are also a very good way to control your speed. Whenever you feel you are going too fast, link a few turns together and you will slow down automatically. The two types of turn that you should learn first are the A-frame turn and the parallel turn. Practise in a large area with plenty of room to turn freely.

Keep your head up and your arms just below shoulder height.

Inside edges

Bend this knee slightly more than the other knee.

Inside skate

Outside skate

Keep your shoulders and hips square as you turn.

Your weight should be evenly placed on both feet.

A-frame turn

1 The A-frame turn is an ideal turn to learn first because your feet are wide apart, which makes you more stable. During this turn, your body should resemble a capital "A" shape, hence the name. Learn on a flat surface or a gently sloping hill at first. Glide forwards in an A-stance (see page 17), with your feet wider than your hips. Your weight should be evenly distributed over both feet. Keep your head up and your arms out in front.

2 To turn left, as shown above, bend your right knee slightly more than the left. This will put more pressure on the ball of your right foot and force your right, or outside, skate to turn. To turn right, put more pressure on the left foot.

3 Keep your feet apart and your toes pointing forwards during the turn. If you are on a hill, put more pressure on the outside skate.

Skate style

Before you attempt an A-frame turn, practise standing with your feet wider than your hips and your toes pointing straight ahead. Bend your knees and push your shins against the tongues of your boots. You will be on your inside edges.

Good form
A wide stance, inside edges, bent knees, and a lean from the waist are all crucial to a good A-frame turn.

Corresponding edges

You need to be on your corresponding edges (see page 17) to do a parallel turn. Practise rolling on to your right skate and then the left one. You should also practise leaning your body into the turn.

Steering and support skates

In a parallel turn, the front skate is the steering skate. You should put about 60% of your weight on this skate. The back skate, or support skate, should support about 40% of your weight.

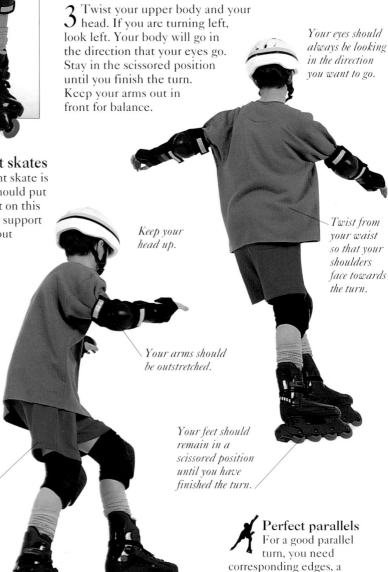

3 Twist your upper body and your head. If you are turning left, look left. Your body will go in the direction that your eyes go. Stay in the scissored position until you finish the turn. Keep your arms out in front for balance.

Your eyes should always be looking in the direction you want to go.

Keep your head up.

Twist from your waist so that your shoulders face towards the turn.

Your arms should be outstretched.

Your feet should remain in a scissored position until you have finished the turn.

Parallel turn

1 Glide forwards with your feet in a scissored position. Most of your weight should be on your front, or steering, skate. Control your speed and make sure you look where you are going.

2 Lean your body into the turn and roll on to your corresponding edges. Your steering skate will be on the outside edge and your support skate on the inside edge.

Lean your entire body into the turn.

Perfect parallels
For a good parallel turn, you need corresponding edges, a scissored stance, and a lean towards the turn.

Keep your knees bent.

Back, or support, skate

Front, or steering, skate

Parallel turns in practice

Parallel turns are not just used in inline skating. This picture shows a skier training on inline skates during the summer months. He is performing a technique called traversing (see page 30). Traversing is one way of going down a hill, executing parallel turns at each side.

Crossover turns

UNLIKE A BASIC TURN, in which you simply coast along as you turn, a crossover turn allows you to maintain and even increase your speed as you turn. Crossovers are a more advanced and efficient way of turning, and they are used a lot in speed skating and inline hockey, where fast changes in direction are essential. If you are right-handed, you will find it easier to turn to the left, and vice versa. However, you should try to be proficient at crossovers to the left and right, so spend time practising on your weaker side, too.

3 Cross your right skate over your left, setting it down on its inside edge just in front of the left skate. At this stage of the crossover, your thighs should be crossed and your left skate will be rolling on its outside edge, still carving the turn. A deep knee bend will make the stepover easier.

The left foot strokes down to the right for the understroke.

4 At the same time as you perform the stepover, you can also do an understroke. The understroke is one of the most powerful and efficient strokes in skating, and the best way to increase your speed. Push your left skate underneath your body, in the opposite direction that you would normally push when stroking and gliding.
 In this picture, the leg is stroking underneath the body to the right.

Set the right skate down on its inside edge.

Skate style
To avoid getting your skates tangled up during the crossover, make sure that the toe of the stepover skate is pointed in the direction of the turn.

Street turns
Mastering crossover turns will help you avoid obstacles in the street while still maintaining your speed. This skater's deep knee bend, and the way his legs are crossed at the thighs, help make the stepover much easier.

Pick up this foot and replace it in the position shown in step one.

Bending your knees and leaning into the turn will help you turn much faster.

Right turn
When turning to the right, simply reverse these instructions, substituting right for left and left for right.

5 When you have completed the stepover and understroke, put your weight on your right skate (the stepover skate) and pick up your left skate (your understroke skate). Move this skate back to the original position on its outside edge, ready to repeat with another stepover.

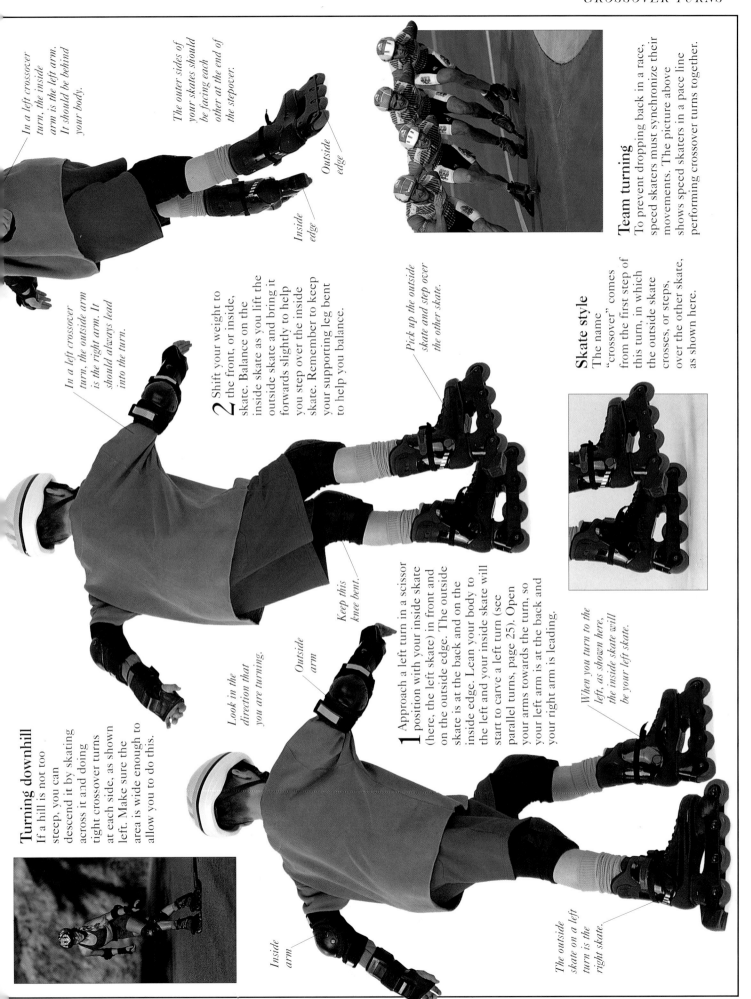

In a left crossover turn, the inside arm is the left arm. It should be behind your body.

The outer sides of your skates should be facing each other at the end of the stepover.

Outside edge

Inside edge

Team turning
To prevent dropping back in a race, speed skaters must synchronize their movements. The picture above shows speed skaters in a pace line performing crossover turns together.

In a left crossover turn, the outside arm is the right arm. It should always lead into the turn.

2 Shift your weight to the front, or inside, skate. Balance on the inside skate as you lift the outside skate and bring it forwards slightly to help you step over the inside skate. Remember to keep your supporting leg bent to help you balance.

Pick up the outside skate and step over the other skate.

Skate style
The name "crossover" comes from the first step of this turn, in which the outside skate crosses, or steps, over the other skate, as shown here.

Keep this knee bent.

Outside arm

Look in the direction that you are turning.

1 Approach a left turn in a scissor position with your inside skate (here, the left skate) in front and on the outside edge. The outside skate is at the back and on the inside edge. Lean your body to the left and your inside skate will start to carve a left turn (see parallel turns, page 25). Open your arms towards the turn, so your left arm is at the back and your right arm is leading.

Turning downhill
If a hill is not too steep, you can descend it by skating across it and doing tight crossover turns at each side, as shown left. Make sure the area is wide enough to allow you to do this.

When you turn to the left, as shown here, the inside skate will be your left skate.

Inside arm

The outside skate on a left turn is the right skate.

Skating backwards

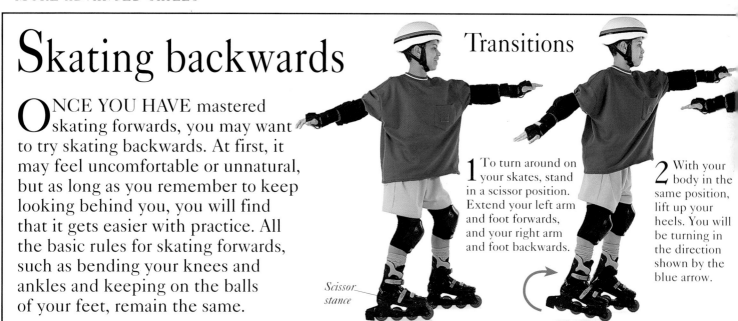

ONCE YOU HAVE mastered skating forwards, you may want to try skating backwards. At first, it may feel uncomfortable or unnatural, but as long as you remember to keep looking behind you, you will find that it gets easier with practice. All the basic rules for skating forwards, such as bending your knees and ankles and keeping on the balls of your feet, remain the same.

Scissor stance

Transitions

1 To turn around on your skates, stand in a scissor position. Extend your left arm and foot forwards, and your right arm and foot backwards.

2 With your body in the same position, lift up your heels. You will be turning in the direction shown by the blue arrow.

Backward crossovers

Before you attempt a backward crossover, you should practise sculling backwards. This involves swizzling with one foot (see page 29) while the other foot glides along the ground. When you feel comfortable sculling backwards on each foot, you will be ready to turn it into a backward crossover. Crossovers are used mainly for turning, so make sure you have a large area in which to practise.

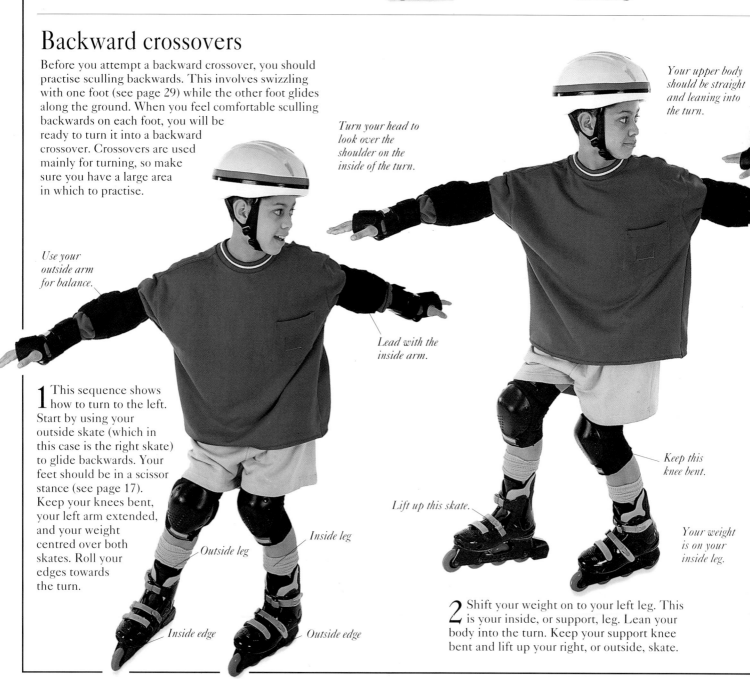

Use your outside arm for balance.

Turn your head to look over the shoulder on the inside of the turn.

Your upper body should be straight and leaning into the turn.

Lead with the inside arm.

1 This sequence shows how to turn to the left. Start by using your outside skate (which in this case is the right skate) to glide backwards. Your feet should be in a scissor stance (see page 17). Keep your knees bent, your left arm extended, and your weight centred over both skates. Roll your edges towards the turn.

Outside leg

Inside leg

Inside edge

Outside edge

Lift up this skate.

Keep this knee bent.

Your weight is on your inside leg.

2 Shift your weight on to your left leg. This is your inside, or support, leg. Lean your body into the turn. Keep your support knee bent and lift up your right, or outside, skate.

Keep your arms in the same position.

3 Quickly pivot on your front wheels, with your toes facing the direction of the turn (see arrow). Your arms and head should not move.

A soft landing
Practise transitions on grass first to avoid injuring yourself.

4 Your heels should now be pointing backwards. Lower them to the ground. Keep your arms and head in the same position and look over your shoulder.

Swizzling backwards

This is like swizzling forwards (see page 19), but because you are going backwards, you must look over your shoulder to see where you are going.

1 From the ready position (see page 17), point your toes inwards so that your feet form an "A" shape on the ground. Twist your upper body so that you can look over your shoulder.

2 Make sure you are on your inside edges and then push both skates outwards at the same time. You should start rolling backwards. Keep your knees bent and your head up.

3 Centre your weight over your skates, and draw your feet together into a "V" shape. Practise this in-out movement until it becomes a natural, flowing sequence.

Remember to look where you are going.

Keep your arms outstretched.

Cross the right skate over the left skate.

Try to land on your inside edge.

3 Cross your right skate over your left skate and set the right skate down on its inside edge. Your legs will be crossed at the thighs. Set the right skate down so that it is parallel to the left skate.

Make sure you have regained your balance before lifting up your left skate.

Changing direction
If you want to turn to the right, simply follow this sequence, substituting left for right and right for left.

4 Transfer your weight to the right skate so that you can pick up the left skate and replace it in a scissor position on the outside edge, ready to do another crossover. Make sure you always point your heels towards the turn.

Pick up your left skate and place it in a scissor position.

Hills and hazards

P ART OF THE CHALLENGE of inline skating outdoors are the unexpected hills and hazards that you will inevitably encounter. A hazard is anything from a twig to a slippery patch of oil. While the safest, easiest way to deal with hazards is to avoid them, this is not always possible. Always analyze a situation before tackling it and never attempt a move that is above your skill or confidence level.

Going downhill

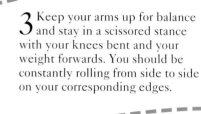

1 Skating down hills can be both challenging and frightening. Before you even attempt a hill, you must be able to control your skates and stop easily at high speeds. You must also consider whether the gradient of the hill is within your skill level.

3 Keep your arms up for balance and stay in a scissored stance with your knees bent and your weight forwards. You should be constantly rolling from side to side on your corresponding edges.

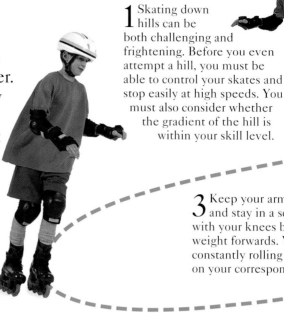

Rail grind
Grinding along rails, above, is part of street skating (see page 34). Stunts like this require special street style skates with plates fitted to the frame.

2 The best way to go downhill is to use a skiing technique called traversing. Traversing involves a series of parallel turns (see page 25) to the right and the left. These allow you to skate across a hill instead of straight down it.

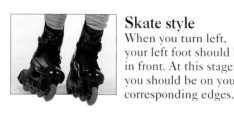

Skate style
When you turn left, your left foot should be in front. At this stage, you should be on your corresponding edges.

Back, or supporting, skate

4 Each time you traverse from side to side, you must put your inside leg in front to lead you into the turn. Your back leg will support you throughout the turn, but you should have more weight on your inside leg.

Front, or inside, skate

Slalom
Try doing parallel turns on one foot through a line of cones, called a slalom. This helps to perfect switching quickly from the inside to the outside edge of the gliding skate.

6 When you approach the bottom of the hill, get ready to use your heel brake (see page 20). If the way ahead is clear, you may want to continue skating forwards.

Skate style
When you turn right, your right skate should be in front to lead into the turn.

Zigzag
Traversing is the safest way to descend a hill, because it allows you to control your speed.

5 If you start to go too fast, turn more and skate uphill slightly. This will quickly reduce your speed.

Up kerbs

When you are skating outdoors, you will probably have to go up and down kerbs at some stage. Once you get the hang of it, hopping up kerbs is simple.

1 Stepping forwards on to a kerb is just like walking. Glide towards the kerb and shift your weight on to one skate, lifting the other skate up.

Keep your weight on this skate.

2 When your front skate is on the kerb, put your weight on to it and lift the back skate up. Glide forwards on the pavement on both skates, keeping your weight forwards.

Step with this skate.

Your weight should be forwards.

The side step

Approaching a kerb from the side is slightly easier because you only need to take a small side step.

1 Glide towards the kerb with your skates in a scissor stance. Your inside leg should be in front. Transfer your weight to your outside leg. Lift up the inside skate and place it on the kerb.

Your weight should be on this skate.

Balancing act
Keep your arms in front to help you balance and look towards the kerb to make sure you have stepped far enough.

2 Put your weight on the upper skate, bend your knees and lift the bottom skate. Set it down in a scissor stance and glide forwards on both skates.

Inside leg

Arms out for balance

Down kerbs

The easiest way to go down a kerb is to stop and step off it, but if you want to keep up your speed, you can just skate off.

Straight upper body

Bend your knees and ankles forwards.

Arms out

1 Approach the kerb in a scissor stance with your heel brake at the back. Keep your weight over your second and third wheels.

2 Simply glide off the kerb. Do not jump. Keep your body in the same position and bend your knees and ankles forwards to absorb the impact of landing.

Over twigs

Try to avoid hazards such as twigs, sticks, or gravel as they can get caught in your skates and make you fall. If you do skate through such things, take small steps and make sure you lift your feet up high.

Lift up your feet to stop twigs from catching in your wheels.

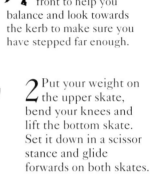
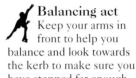

Jumping

WHEN YOU HAVE PERFECTED the basic skating moves and feel confident on your skates, you may want to try more complicated skills. The jump is the main move in a type of skating called extreme skating (see page 34). Extreme skating includes riding stairs, grinding rails, and jumping off launch ramps. It is thrilling to watch and to perform, but it is very difficult and you should never underestimate the risk in doing some of these moves. Try to break down each of the jumps shown here into steps you can practise separately.

Dizzy heights
For experienced skaters, the thrill of jumping on higher ramps or quarter pipes is hard to beat. This picture was taken at the Street finals of the World Championships in Switzerland, and shows me catching some really big air off a high launch ramp!

Jumping with a ramp

You need lots of skill, confidence, and nerve to try this. When you first learn, it's a good idea to ask two friends to help you. They can skate on either side of you, holding lightly onto your hands and supporting you as you ride off the ramp. This will help you to build up the confidence to do it on your own. Always wear full protective gear when attempting any kind of jump.

1 Mark a chalk line 3 m (10 ft) away from the ramp. Build up speed on your approach to the ramp, and then start to glide when you reach the chalk line.

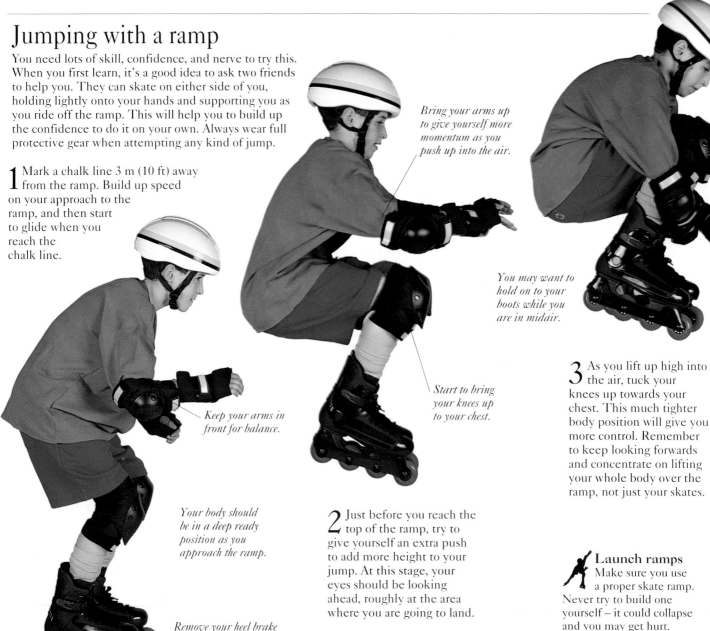

Keep your arms in front for balance.

Your body should be in a deep ready position as you approach the ramp.

Remove your heel brake before attempting any jumps to avoid getting it caught.

Bring your arms up to give yourself more momentum as you push up into the air.

Start to bring your knees up to your chest.

2 Just before you reach the top of the ramp, try to give yourself an extra push to add more height to your jump. At this stage, your eyes should be looking ahead, roughly at the area where you are going to land.

You may want to hold on to your boots while you are in midair.

3 As you lift up high into the air, tuck your knees up towards your chest. This much tighter body position will give you more control. Remember to keep looking forwards and concentrate on lifting your whole body over the ramp, not just your skates.

Launch ramps
Make sure you use a proper skate ramp. Never try to build one yourself – it could collapse and you may get hurt.

Learning to jump

Body position, weight distribution, and speed are the keys to jumping. When you first start jumping, it is a good idea to begin with small jumps before progressing to something bigger. Jump from a standing position to start with and then insert a short glide.

Bring your arms back to provide the momentum that you need to get into the air.

1 Lean forwards from your waist and bend your knees deeply. Pull your arms back.

Stand with your feet in a scissor position.

2 Keeping your body straight, jump up into the air. Bring your arms forwards to help you balance.

Push off from your toes as you lift up into the air.

Remember to keep your head up.

3 Bend your knees when you land. Make sure your feet are in the scissor position.

Let your knees start to drop from their tucked position.

Start to move your feet into a scissor position.

4 At the height of your jump, you will start to drop down towards the ground. Lower your knees slightly from the tucked position and start to scissor your feet.

A heavy landing
The higher you jump, the heavier you will land, so always make sure that you bend your knees when you land to avoid injury.

Look at your landing point, not your skates.

6 When you land, try to bend your knees deeply to absorb the impact of hitting the ground. Keep your feet in the scissor position and your arms in front as you glide forwards. Make sure you are properly balanced before you start striding forwards again.

5 Extend your legs and position your strongest foot at the back of the scissor position to give you better balance and support. Try landing with first your right foot behind you and then your left foot, to discover which one feels the most stable and comfortable.

Your strongest leg is behind.

Keep your knees bent.

Other inline events

THERE IS MUCH MORE to inline skating than simply skating around a park or rink. Once you have worked on the fundamental skills and feel really confident, you may want to use these as a basis for trying different aspects of skating. It is often a good idea to join a club that specializes in a specific type of skating, because it will offer expert coaching, as well as the chance to compete against other people and make new friends. No matter which skating activity you choose, it will keep you fit, healthy, and active for years to come!

Skate-to-ski

Inline skating is very similar to skiing. This makes skating ideal for ski training during the summer months, when there is no snow around. The picture above shows an inline skater practising the "tuck" position for ski racing. You should be confident about travelling downhill quickly before you try this.

Inline racing

Most races take place during the spring and summer. The most popular distance is the 10-km (6.2-miles) race. The speed skating stance shown below requires a lot of practice, and it is a good idea to join a club and get some expert coaching. In addition to advice on technique, you will benefit from tips on where to position yourself at the start of a large inline race (above), how to pace yourself, and when to sprint towards the finish.

Extreme, or street, skating

Tricks or stunts such as jumping off ramps (above) and riding stairs are part of extreme skating. Extreme skating is exciting but dangerous. As well as full protective gear, you should have special stunt skates with grind plates and power straps.

Speed skating

Speed skaters adopt a very low skating position, with their knees bent to almost 90 degrees. They let their arms swing from side to side in big arcs (shown left), or keep their hands behind their backs. Because of the high speeds they reach, speed skaters must wear helmets and wrist guards, but do without knee and elbow pads as these restrict movement.

Rail grinding

Grind plates are fitted to skates to help them slide and protect the frame from damage (above).

Jumps

Jumps can be set up anywhere with a clear approach and landing area. Make sure the jump is not too high for you.

Inline hockey

Inline hockey has its roots in traditional ice hockey. The inline skates that we know today were developed by ice-hockey players looking for a way to play during the summer months. Inline hockey has now become an established sport in its own right, and its players are among the most accomplished inline skaters. Like ice hockey, inline hockey is played with a weighted puck and wooden hockey sticks, and the winning team is the one which puts the puck into their opponent's net the most times.

However, unlike ice hockey, inline hockey can be played on virtually any large, flat area. It requires five players rather than the traditional six, and because it is much faster and more physically demanding than ice hockey, it is played in two 15-minute halves. Most adult hockey teams have children's teams, and there are also children's leagues. You should always wear full protective gear, and ideally have skates that are specifically designed for inline hockey.

Glossary

You may be unfamiliar with many of the terms used by inline skaters. Some of the more common ones are listed below.

A

A-frame A wide stance used to start turning movements. Helps to maintain balance and a low centre of gravity.

Allen key A tool used to unscrew the bolts that hold the wheels and the brake in place.

B

Bearing A case containing seven ball bearings that are shielded and pre-packed in grease. This reduces friction and allows the wheels to spin smoothly.

Brake The rubber stop usually found on the right skate. Brakes can be either round or square.

C

Centre of gravity The distribution of weight that keeps you evenly balanced. It is crucial to maintain your centre of gravity if you are to avoid falling.

Crossover An advanced turning technique, usually used by skaters turning at greater speeds.

D

Diameter The size of the skate wheels. It is measured in millimetres.

Duck walk A method of walking for beginners in which the feet are turned out.

Durometer A term for measuring the hardness of a skate wheel. Ranges from 74A–93A. The higher the number, the harder the wheel.

E

Edges The side and centre of the skate wheels. They allow you to turn and stop.

Elbow/knee pads Protective safety equipment with reinforced plastic and foam to protect the elbow and knee joints in a fall.

F

Frame The part of your skate underneath your boot which holds the wheels in place.

Freestyle General term for dancing movements.

G

Grind plate A metal frame that fits on to the skate frame to prevent frame damage and help the sliding action when grinding.

H

Helmet The most important part of your protective gear. Made with an inner shock absorption layer and an outer protective shell.

I

Inside skate The skate that is closest to a turn.

K

Knee pads *see* Elbow pads

M

Momentum The force with which you travel forwards.

O

Outside skate The skate that is outside or away from a turn.

P

Parallel turn An advanced method of turning using corresponding wheel edges.

Power slide A way of stopping while travelling backwards. Used by inline hockey players.

Power strap An additional buckle to tighten the cuff or the top of a skate.

Puck In inline hockey, a weighted disc or ball that players try to put into their opponent's goal.

Q

Quad skate Refers to the original, four-wheeled skate.

R

Ramp A wooden or metal structure used to get air, or jump. Usually 1–1.5 m (3–5 ft) high.

Rockering Lowering the middle skate wheels to create a curved wheel line. Allows a skater to make quicker turns.

Rotation Inline wheels should be rotated to enhance their performance and make them last longer, especially when performing wheel-grinding stopping techniques such as the T-stop.

S

Slalom Involves weaving in and out of evenly-spaced markers in a line.

Spacer A plastic or metal device in the centre of the wheel to prevent the bearings from making contact with each other.

Stance The way to stand on inline skates.

Swizzling A technique of skating in which skates are moved in and out while never leaving the ground. This creates an hour-glass path on the ground.

T

T-stop A braking technique in which the non-lead leg is placed at the back of the leading leg to form a capital "T" shape, applying friction between the inner edges of the wheels and the ground.

W

Wrist guard Protective handwear that minimizes injury to the wrists and palms, usually the first areas to hit the ground in a fall. A plastic bar usually runs from the bottom of the wrist across the palm of the hand.

Index

Useful addresses

These inline skating organizations and suppliers may be able to give you more information on skating clubs and coaches.

International Inline Skating Association (IISA)
PO Box 15482
Atlanta, GA, 30333, United States

British Inline Skating Association (BISA)
Suite 479, 2 Old Brompton Road
London SW3 3DQ

British Federation of Roller Skating (BFRS)
4 Windsor Road
Castle Bromwich
Birmingham B36 0JN

British Skater Hockey Association (BSHA)
Grammont
Chiddingly Road
Horam, Heathfield
East Sussex TN21 0JH

Fagans (Bauer)
Unit 4B, Kingston House Estate
Portsmouth Road
Thames Ditton
Surrey KT6 5QB

Europasport (Rollerblade®)
Ann Street
Kendal, Cumbria, LA9 6AA

Force 10 (K2)
91 Ashenden Walk
Tunbridge Wells
Kent TN2 3UJ

Magazines:
Skatermag
The Blue Barn, Tew Lane
Wootton, Woodstock
Oxon OX20 1HA

1st Inline Magazine
4th Floor
The Fitzpatrick Building
188 York Way
London N7 9QR

Kelly Simeon Peter James Barry Lee

Acknowledgments

Dorling Kindersley would like to thank the following people
for their kind help in the production of this book:

With special thanks to Dawn Irwin, IISA instructor, for her expert advice at the photo sessions and her technical input into the book; all the Young Inline Skaters for their skill and enthusiasm during the photography; Sarah McClurey for her technical advice at the photo shoot for pages 14/15, and her continued input into this series; Aldie Chalmers and Lesley Kendrick for their support and enthusiasm throughout this project; Tom Chant at Fagans, UK distributors of Bauer inline skates and Cooper hockey equipment; Ray Moller and Tim Kelly for their patience during the photography; Jacques Ouwerx of BISA for his advice; The Queen Mother Sports Centre for their hospitality.

Picture credits
Key: c=centre; b=bottom; r=right; l=left; t=top.

Action Plus Photographic / Steve Bardens; 34br; Davis Barber: 35tl; Sandy Chalmers / Inline Skatermag, Oxon: 21br, crb; Tony Donaldson: 8cl, br, 26br; Mary Evans Picture Library: 9tl, cl, c, b; The Image Bank: 18cl; 19cr / Marc Romanelli: 34t, bl; Thorsten Indra: 8tl, bl; 30bl; 34cr, bc; Mountain Stock Photography and Film, Inc / Chaco Mohler: 27bl / Nagel: 25br; Anne Marie Weber: 27tr; Michael Reusse: 8cr; 30cl; Rollerblade® Inc: 9cr, br / Featuring Geo Rollerblade® Team / Michael Voorhees: 34cl.
Jacket: Paul Rickleton: back bl; Thorsten Indra: front tl, Inside back t.
Endpapers: Mountain Stock Photography / Leighton White.